Noah and the great flood

Story by Penny Frank

Illustrated by Tony Morris

THE LION
STORY BIBLE

3

OXFORD · BATAVIA · SYDNEY

The Bible tells us that when God made the world, everything was good. He made the earth and the animals and the people. But the people disobeyed him and spoiled the world. Time passed and things became so bad that God was sorry he had ever made people. But there was one man he was pleased with. His name was Noah. You can find the story in your own Bible, in Genesis, starting at chapter 6.

Copyright © 1986 Lion Publishing

Published by
Lion Publishing plc
Sandy Lane West, Littlemore, Oxford, England
ISBN 0 85648 728 7
ISBN 0 7459 1748 8 (paperback)
Lion Publishing Corporation
1705 Hubbard Avenue, Batavia, Illinois 60510, USA
ISBN 0 85648 728 7
Albatross Books Pty Ltd
PO Box 320, Sutherland, NSW 2232, Australia
ISBN 0 86760 512 X
ISBN 0 7324 0068 8 (paperback)

First edition 1986, reprinted 1987, 1988
Paperback edition 1989

British Library Cataloguing in Publication Data

Frank, Penny
  Noah and the great flood. –
  (The Lion Story Bible; 3)
  1. Noah's ark – Juvenile literature
  2. Bible stories, English – O.T.
  Genesis
  I. Title   II. Morris, Tony
  222'.1109505   BS580.N6

ISBN 0-85648-728-7
ISBN 0-7459-1748-8 (paperback)

Printed in Yugoslavia

Library of Congress Cataloging in Publication Data

Frank, Penny.
  Noah and the great flood.
  (The Lion Story Bible; 3)
  1. Noah's ark – Juvenile literature.
  2. Noah (Biblical figure) – Juvenile
  literature. 3. Bible stories,
  English – O.T. Genesis. [1. Noah
  (Biblical figure). 2. Noah's ark. 3. Bible
  stories – O.T.] I. Morris, Tony, ill.
  II. Title. III. Series: Frank, Penny.
  Lion Story Bible; 3.
  BS658.F73 1986   222'.1109505
  85-13158
  ISBN 0-85648-728-7
  ISBN 0-7459-1748-8 (paperback)

When God first made the world, everything was good. But soon God was sad when he saw the people he had put in his beautiful world. They were not the way he had made them. They were unkind. They hurt one another. They did not even try to obey God any more.

God was sad — and he was angry.

3

'The people who have disobeyed me must be punished,' God said. 'I shall send a great flood to wash the earth clean. My world will be as it was when I first made it. I shall begin all over again.'

There was just one man on earth who was God's friend. He was a good man, and God was pleased with him. His name was Noah.

God told Noah what he was going to do. But he promised that Noah and his family would be safe.

'I have an important job for you to do,'
God told Noah. 'You will need to build
an enormous boat. You will be safe
inside while I wash the earth clean.'

God told Noah exactly how to build the special boat.

It had many rooms, a roof, a window, and a door in the side. God told Noah to make it from strong wood and to paint it with tar to keep out all the water.

Noah worked hard. He had never made
a boat before but God told him just what
to do.

When it was finished Noah took his
whole family inside. They made sure
they had all the food they needed.

God said to Noah, 'You must take into
the boat a pair of all the birds and
animals I have made. You must look
after them while the earth is made
clean, so make sure you have the food
each animal likes.'

8

Noah and his family made the animals comfortable in the rooms of the boat. They stored away the food they needed.

When everything in the boat was as God wanted it, God shut the door of the boat.

The people who had disobeyed him were left outside.

Then God sent the rain.

The rain came in a storm. It made a terrible noise on the roof of the boat. And it went on and on.

Slowly the water rose. The boat began to float on the water.

It rained for a long time.

The animals wanted to get out and run on the grass.

Noah's family wanted to live in a house again.

But Noah said, 'You must wait.'

After many days the rain stopped. The water was so deep it covered even the mountain-tops.

Then the wind began to blow and the boat drifted on the water.

The wind blew — and the water began
to go down.

One day Noah's family could see the
mountain-tops poking up out of the
water.

Noah said, 'The birds need to stretch their wings. I will send out a raven.'

The raven flew off and did not come back. Then Noah sent out a dove, but the dove came back quickly. She could not find a dry place to rest.

The next time Noah sent out the dove
she found a tree peeping up through the
water. She broke off a twig with green
leaves and took it back to the boat.

One day the boat bumped onto some dry ground. The great flood was over.

Noah said, 'God has kept his promise. The earth will soon be dry enough for us to live on. I will send out the dove again. Perhaps she will find a place to live.'

When the dove did not come back, Noah knew that the water had gone and the earth was dry.

God said to Noah, 'My world is ready
for you again. Bring out your family
and all the animals.'

Noah and his family enjoyed being in
the fresh air.

They stood together to say thank you
to God for keeping them safe in the
flood. They thanked God for his
beautiful world.

21

'I am sad that I had to flood my earth and wash away the people and good things I had made,' said God. 'I want you to live happy lives in my world. Look!'

They looked up and saw a beautiful shining rainbow.

'Whenever you see a rainbow,' said God, 'remember that I have promised never again to send a flood like this one. You know that I always keep my promises.'

The Lion Story Bible is made up of 52 individual stories for young readers, building up an understanding of the Bible as one story — God's story — a story for all time and all people.

The Old Testament section (numbers 1–30) tells the story of a great nation — God's chosen people, the Israelites — and God's love and care for them through good times and bad. The stories are about people who knew and trusted God. From this nation came one special person, Jesus Christ, sent by God to save all people everywhere.

The story of *Noah and the great flood* comes from the first book of the Bible, Genesis, chapters 6–9.

God is just and good, but the people God made chose to disobey him. They spoiled his good world and became more and more evil. God cannot let evil go unchecked. The flood was his judgment on mankind. But he is also loving and very patient. So he saved Noah and his family and made a new start possible.

He also makes promises, which he always keeps. The story of Noah is a story of judgment, justly deserved, and of promise. The rainbow, which we often see when rain comes, is a lovely reminder of the promise God made never again to destroy all life on earth in a flood.

The next story in this series, number 4: *Abraham, friend of God*, tells how God chose one of Noah's descendants to be the founder of a very special nation.